My Very MONSTER

Book of SHAPES

Written and Illustrated by
Tim Read

My Very Silly Monster
Book of Shapes
Text copyright ©2015 Tim Read
Illustration copyright ©2015 Tim Read

ISBN-13: 978-1511489805
ISBN-10: 1511489804

To: NORA !! Be Silly!!

Special Thanks to Emily Beaudry for setting me straight and lending her geometric expertise to this project.

Visit us at:
www.MyVerySillyMonster.com

For Barb
Thanks for always keeping this square in good shape.
-TR

Dear Very Silly Monster Parents,

Welcome to *My Very Silly Monster Book of Shapes*!

In this book are twenty-two fun and colorful Very Silly Monsters ready to teach your child all about shapes. Your child will enjoy learning about basic shapes such as *Circle, Square, and Triangle*. They also learn about more complex shapes such as *Rhombus and Pentagon*.

Although many of the shape names are challenging to read and pronounce this is not actually a reading book but rather an introduction to the wonderful world of shapes. I encourage you to go through each page with your child and explore the shapes as you read each name aloud one by one. Included are colorful illustrations of every day items to accompany each shape to give an example of how shapes are a part of our everyday lives. Below are some tips on how to get the most out of *My Very Silly Monster Book of Shapes*.

1. Have your child trace each shape with their finger to get a sense of how a shape is formed.

2. Count and discuss the number of sides each shape has, and how they are different from similar looking shapes.

3. Notice how each Very Silly Monster has a shape of their own.

4. After reading this book with your child, look around your home and see if they can spot any of the shapes from the book.

5. Ask your child to draw their own Monster Shape and give it a clever name. Make up a silly story about how it became the shape it has chosen.

6. Most of all, enjoy the time you spend with your child looking at the illustrations and ask them to tell you which Very Silly Monster shape is their favorite and why.

Thanks and enjoy *My Very Silly Monster Book of Shapes!*
Peace,
Tim Read

Cecil's
Circle

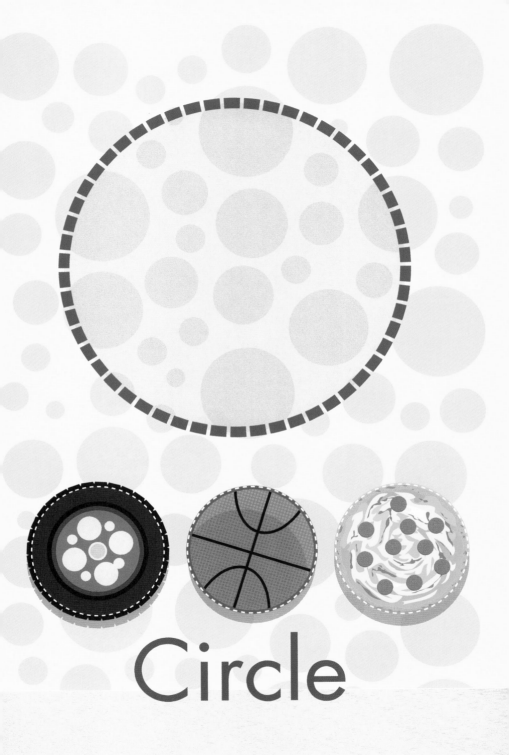

Circle

Eli's Ellipse

Ellipse

Squiggie's Square

Square

Ovi's Oval

Oval

Reggie's Rectangle

Rectangle

Trinity's Triangle

Triangle

Trudy's Trapezoid

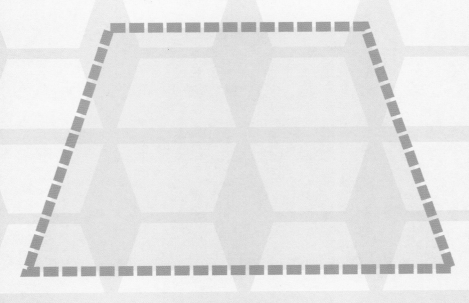

Trapezoid

Paddy's Parallelogram

Parallelogram

Rhonda's Rhombus

Rhombus
(Diamond)

Henley's Hexagon

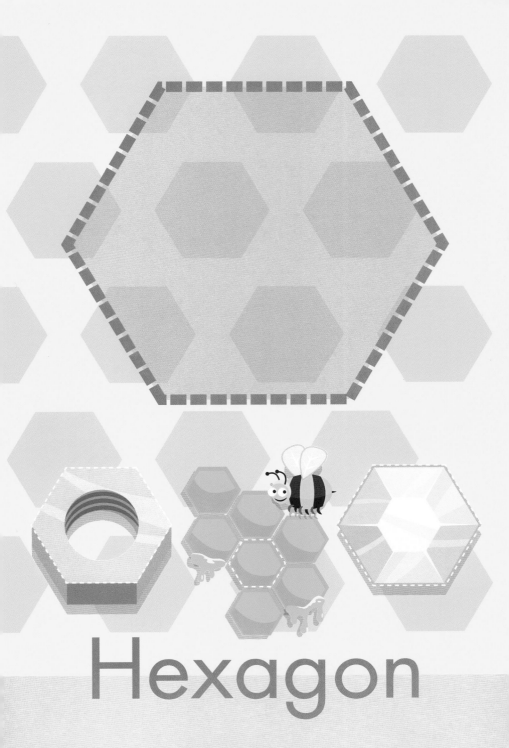

Hexagon

Octavia's Octagon

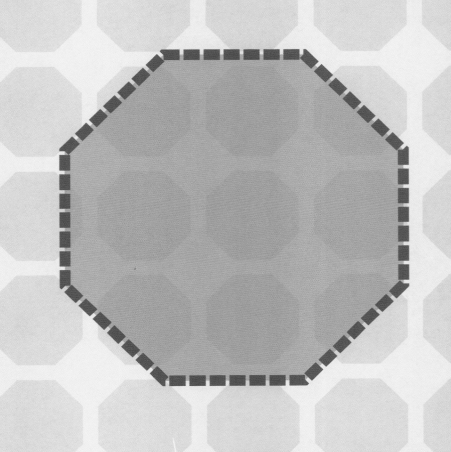

Octagon

Petunia's Pentagon

Pentagon

Harold's
Heart

Heart

Kyle's Kite

Kite

MORE SILLY SHAPES TO LEARN!

FIND THE SHAPE ON THE OPPOSITE PAGE THAT MATCHES *MY VERY SILLY MONSTER* SHAPE FRIENDS.

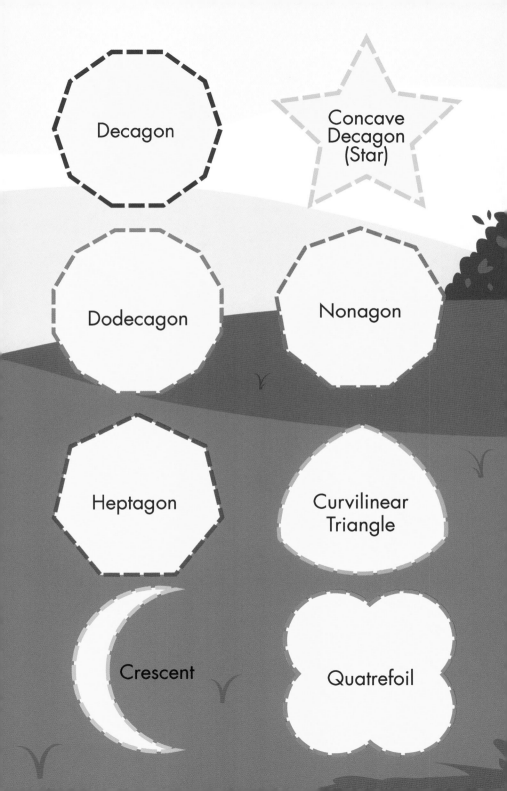

Decagon

Concave
Decagon
(Star)

Dodecagon

Nonagon

Heptagon

Curvilinear
Triangle

Crescent

Quatrefoil

How to draw
The Ellipse Very Silly Monster

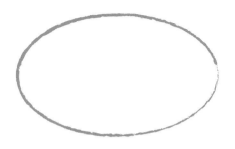

Draw an ellipse.

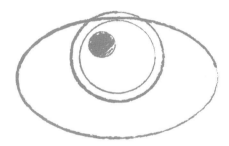

**Draw an eye.
(or a few eyes)**

**Add feet
and some hair.**

Finish by adding toes, spots, and a mouth. Don't forget the teeth!

When you're done, color your creation and hang it up for everyone to enjoy.

Awesome!

Made in the USA
Charleston, SC
21 November 2015